sacramental sonnets

sacramental sonnets

a poem cycle

1982

alison bielski

ALUN BOOKS
2003

acknowledgements

Anglo-Welsh Review, Acumen, Element Five, Poet's Voice, Moorlands Review, Doors of Dorset, Orbis Poems for Peace (prizewinner), Western Mail.
The Crimson Flame: selected poems, edited by Fred Beake (Mammon Press) for University of Salzburg

ISBN 0 907117 89 9

Typeset in 11/13pt Arial

Printed in Great Britain by
Andreas Haaf & Son, Port Talbot
Bound by Principal Bookbinders, Ystradgynlais

1.
advent letter

each year I write to you at advent time
packing events of months upon pale pages
these ritual phrases always stay the same
for I omit my life's unfolding stages
yet starting 'dearest' words begin to flow
making each paragraph a sacrament
I retrace fields upon this patch of snow
my pen explores our curving lanes of Gwent
we tried to sever links but still retained
a shared experience that would not die
tentative letters passed for there remained
harmony neither of us could destroy
each year the relics are unlocked then we
post our white envelopes replace the key

2.
reply

this Christmas morning through my letter-flap
a storm of whiteness tumbles to dark floor
letters lie upside-down in a rough heap
I gather all these wishes from my door
turn over envelopes in hope and fear
postmarks revealing what I need to know
then suddenly your level hand appears
on one wide rectangle of even snow
the written sacrament has been prepared
I slit your offering with olive wood
then elevate this wafer pale as bread
drawing out pages written in bright blood
I eat and drink each loving word you write
standing transfigured in your sudden light

3.
St. Julian's chapel Tenby

waves lashing this harbour crash on shore
flooding quay steps while stumbling we descend
with watchful fishermen who eased the door
to pray for safety before leaving land
inside their anchored chapel of Welsh stone
where warmth and brightness insulate from cold
we hear the single bell's last hollow tone
and gaze on altar sails of threaded gold
blackness of winter evening prowls outside
but cannot smother windows of this ark
the sacrament is raised above high tide
wafer and wine hold back the pounding dark
our outflung ropes of faith now knotted fast
steady the rocking cross upon the mast

4.
new year

to mark that passage of our vanished year
we lift full glasses high in mellow light
wish festival goodwill and gentle care
would still remain in january's night
our quarrelling and bitterness in store
will soon be shaken upon dusty air
for wrapped in selfish worries as before
we all forget the human need to share
yet when our gale-blown days give way to snow
and we must feel its slowly falling cold
we shall become good neighbours as we go
on simple errands for the ill and old
fresh footprints leaving trails of living deeds
over thick snow that hides perennial weeds

5.
snowbound in Dyfed

no water as the great freeze locks its grip
so struggling home with one new loaf of bread
that bald announcement echoes while I slip
and stumble on this uncleared frozen road
scraping my balcony I scoop cold snow
into a plastic bucket with small trowel
heat white-filled saucepans on the cooker's glow
to wash essential clothes in steaming bowl
I boil snow coffee carry coloured mugs
hearing the helicopter's rattling drone
announcing food supplies then surging plugs
celebrate electricity's return
upon my desk this sonnet waits complete
calming the chaos of our snowbound street

6.
apricots in january

these wrinkled fragments packaged tidily
are orange god-flesh cut and placed on show
I buy dried fruit of the precocious tree
while shopping in pale january snow
ripened and picked in sunshine of last year
their soaking skins swell gently as they gleam
from glowing honey gold ambrosia
offered to mortals in a steady stream
I stand this copper pan on a low flame
each bubble bursts releasing heady scent
when cooled I eat soft morsels gently drain
their heady liquid feeling confident
that I am sipping slowly flowing spring
gaining new strength this sacrament must bring

7.
Christingle

hold your ripe orange to portray the world
cut out one silver star for earth's north pole
let scarlet ribbon in a girdle curl
under white candle pressed into deep hole
pierce skin with pointed sticks and gently thread
sultanas on straight branches light the flame
carry your bright Christingle as you tread
swift-darkened aisles in this crowded dream
spilt blood and wounding spear are still unknown
to boys and girls who climb up crimson stairs
fruits from thin soil picked by a ragged train
of third world workers wrinkle in despair
envying innocence each parent stands
sees altar steps blaze beneath thrusting hands

8.
sanctuary

crossing the threshold of my curtained room
where desk waits ready with attendant chair
now I intrude to dissipate the gloom
and fill this sanctuary with light and air
each paper is replaced as it was found
mute tape-recorder pens and pencils stare
with shocked hostility at dust-free ground
waste paper rattles in its caged despair
nothing must be disturbed especially those
ideas that hang as cobwebs from each lamp
these heavy books I do not dare to close
whose references hide in spotted damp
my publications ranged along each shelf
command this scene more real than myself

9.
Tenby after snow

how grey is landscape after snow has thawed
salted sand scatters traces over stone
hollows and ruts scar every tarmac road
dead thrushes rot to brittle yellow bone
machines have raised a mound of blackened snow
in Tudor Square to overflow each drain
the beach quickly regains its sandy glow
for leaden sea lets nothing pale remain
only cliff gardens flaunt their startling green
of glossy leaf and first emerging grass
we search for movement in this coloured scene
small signs that winter's grip begins to ease
under one hedge strong spears break soft earth
white snowdrops startle with their sudden birth

10.
first hyacinths

when snow melts columns of curved bells emerge
thrusting to unexpected winter sun
upon tight crowns that rivetted this verge
of mossy grass colours from springtime stun
long lacquered leaves widen at crimson tip
as foil to stripes that delicately thread
these curling surfaces to open lip
where perfume is released around each head
out of our wilderness of pallid snow
new-stirring poems burst into young year
we saw the shortest day glimmer and go
with festival then january's despair
now marvel at fresh cadences' strong swell
first hyacinths extend their trembling spell

11.
service of unity

the minister in clear decisive voice
proclaims her true equality with men
she offers up our urgent prayers for peace
then leads the singing as we rise again
row upon row of congregation brought
from every church within this gated town
I am surrounded ill-at-ease yet caught
in the enthusiasm loudly shown
we never kneel or cross ourselves but speak
simple responses without rising chant
no cadences surge grandly over bleak
walls where the wooden cross stands vigilant
ritual has been banished and I long
for lingering symbols in that latin tongue

12.
thoughts on my daughter’s birthday

at two a.m. police enter my hall
‘your daughter has been injured in a crash’
I blink away blank menace of their call
snatch clothes and handbag in one lucid flash
start up cold car drive shattered into night
struggling as horror clutches at my throat
now reach the hospital conceal this fright
of passing you unrecognised remote
drugged under bruises you extend one hand
speechless in terror we communicate
silently by that mother-daughter bond
I stagger out quite inarticulate
in spring you limp towards our shaggy lawn
release my arm stand suddenly reborn

13.
quarry

we hunt our prey with torches every night
storing revenge for this malicious girl
Proserpine must stop her dangerous rite
for murderous spring can never be unfurled
in bunkers underground she slyly lingers
with missile button and a length of fuse
forming with her red insistent fingers
flowers of flesh blue as a raging bruise
outwitting us she calculates destruction
with radio-active vengeance breaks our snare
then to avoid lethal contamination
she works in tunnels breathing filtered air
slippery as a spy she weighs our fate
we block all exits let her suffocate

14.
the brevity of love

now love comes riding on a donkey's back
through crowds that gentle sense is passing by
emotion quickens blood beat as I take
your wrist and raise joined fingers to bright sky
palm leaves lie carpeting this dusty ground
our view is blocked so triumph cannot last
near future presses with its raging pain
meeting that promise threaded through the past
we carry fronds to celebrate our love
treading upon the sacramental way
where only present has so much to give
we cannot see beyond this brief display
four days remain then agonising death
will change our living overwhelm the earth

15.
spring offensive

San Salvador numbers its murdered dead
Poland mourns prisoners who disappear
guerillas watch an Afghan mountain road
so savage spring advances everywhere
the British task force heads rapidly west
bearing its youth and arsenal of war
upon a green hill gruesome death took place
changing all history with shocking power
we gather early primroses for church
to decorate stone pillars with bright sun
massed daffodils rise trembling as they catch
wind upon graves where caring hands have come
this raging season overturns calm cold
dangerous spring with running feet of gold

16.
the harrying

now we believe in hell for it remains
with padlocked gate and furnace in the mind
when sinking through cavernous pits of pain
we gasp like Langland horrified to find
slow shrieking words and burning cadences
fighting each other for their brief release
Christlike we tear at chains cause violence
to change to glory and a brilliant peace
our candles are extinguished with that rage
as shimmering we climb out of deep grave
words slowly quiver soon to stain the page
while fading weals of anguish heal and leave
one angel touches blue unfocussed eyes
of this new being then the poem cries

17.
Easter white

white sky and lightening sea under white mist
watch one great boulder roll across his grave
where neatly folded clothes shout emptiness
at that bright figure treading milky waves
cold dew on daisies mirrors petalled white
cream lilies rise in church from windowsills
linen awaits the sacramental rite
heaped wafers marking out this holy meal
triumphant hymns sung by each white-robed child
leap from pale pages over choir stalls
Good Friday darkness scattered by new life
as on neat heads the silver sunlight falls
crossing white sand to walk on springing grass
he scatters whiteness from his radiant face

18.
Easter rising

on Easter monday rise upon this chair
wearing your dress of ribbons and white lace
each driven nail becomes one crimson flower
wide purple sash binds up the sacrifice
now as we kiss your lips so coldly pale
offer us silver coins to put you down
for hidden Judas waits to see you fall
counting as pieces rattle in his palm
our fiddler plays inviting all to dance
but it is time to choose your ruling king
new risen and alive then as we glance
at thorns they vanish under buds of spring
your chair that formed a cross is dragged away
so leave to celebrate this holiday

19.
regeneration

nearing this island in one blackened cloud
an ancient eagle skims over our hill
clawing a clustered branch of scarlet fruit
stains water with pulp and eats its fill
plunges into the lake's turbulent heart
splashing and shaking off age and decay
emerges as a youthful-plumaged bird
surveys light skyline soars towards new day
below grey cliffs we crowd this Celtic shore
our baptism no myth but rite of love
flowing water covers our old despair
no eagle circles but one gentle dove
renewed reborn we smooth each drying limb
sunrise bathes ripples in first crimson gleam

20.
wedding

after our spoken vows you will receive
this golden ring I give to you at last
traditionally it will interweave
with Mary's carved encircling amethyst
your ivory dress and gently falling veil
hold fleeting triumph in this wedding rite
white roses open tumbling in display
to mass over the threshold of delight
after iced cake champagne and telegrams
we leave our families with nervous tears
waving again before the train door slams
upon past carelessness of single years
through bramble-covered hills we rush in rain
the sudden sunshine floods one field of grain

21.
love's illusion

your serpent train wriggles towards the hill
at home again I find a loving presence
on cups and plates wild flowers opening still
quickly made bed holding that faint essence
of every movement made during your stay
until you packed each neatly folded garment
my mind begins to paint from memory
a water-colour without temperament
months later when we meet to touch and kiss
excitement frames this likeness lavishly
soon I am used to gentle tenderness
counting small faults as failings jar on me
flesh conquers spirit and I smash my dream
we are too human never what we seem

22.
bluebell month

when bells merge in a ground-smothering cloud
woodland is blue for Mary's month of may
observe her sky-bright robe falling in folds
to cover glades where spring walks silently
on that azure day before ascension-tide
you vanished over the flower-misted slope
raising your pallid arms in first sunlight
abandoning me without promise or hope
what loneliness filled shadows as I stood
waiting for your return which never came
you left only your essence in this wood
with mocking flowers to carry slowly home
I wrap dead bluebells hiding their decay
the empty vase is dried and put away

23.
harbour rite

one yellow crane noisily fills this hill
descends to harbour quay stacked far below
with blue and scarlet boats each painted hull
waiting for grappling chains to fasten prow
and stern then raise its hollow body high
gull-poised to hang heavily over sea
these fishing craft are lowered into tide
and engine clatter echoes round the bay
soon every boat floats anchored in its place
three rows of nylon ropes spaced evenly
litter of wooden chocks is stacked and space
marked out for cars on may day's holiday
that fuming crane climbs slowly through the town
leaves spring-bright boats rocking in yellow sun

24.
Whitsun lovepoem

separately we lead our routine lives
each so aware of loss but saying nothing
about our parting and those turning knives
gouging away such brief and hasty loving
I watch full moon float over surging water
which separates our darkened promontories
two lands two houses then remember laughter
long conversations and our whispered cries
under my reading lamp I turn white pages
to find the poem we discovered scan
each line marking one day one week those ages
all lovers count before they touch again
suddenly tongues of silver fill my hair
your rushing spirit tumbles through the air

25.
the tyranny of pain

when pain obliterates each waking hour
nothing can penetrate such agony
fighting against enveloping despair
we struggle up through dazing waves to see
white-sheeted bed and marshalled medicines
defying our ability to move
and carry on our normal swift routine
while we equate inaction with reproof
impatience fades when drugs stifle each sense
then endless hours to think and to create
bring disillusion as mind's impotence
ensures that we must dream exist and wait
for that fierce energy that fuels the brain
to nourish every dormant poem with flame

26.
rededication of a memorial window

sunlight shimmers through the living green
four soldier martyrs in tree's rippling branches
George Alban Oswald Edmund saints who shine
above John's text of greater love while France
brings Louis Joan of Arc with Tenby's turn
taken by Julian raising his gold oar
then Nicholas who guides all travellers
journeying over southern Pembrokeshire
this tree twines slowly through our daily lives
while radiant Jesus shows us hope of peace
as men fight on in barren Falkland isles
we draw new strength from Anne and Mary's grace
longing for summer's leaves to greet those men
returning safely to our seaside town

27.
trinity flower

three-petalled trinity your flower crown
glistens each day to show one vivid bud
mystical triangle of earth sky man
you can survive in sunlight or moist shade
snatched from Virginia you spread and thrive
covering corners by perennial store
of shiny stems and striped rush-pointed leaves
above massed roots that hold survival power
neglected for three centuries you fill
derelict gardens with quick jointed growth
spiderwort creeping slenderly on silk
you spin rich purple white or carmine-rose
thought will and feeling form each triple bloom
we dig out muddled weeds to give you room

28.
the naming

Celts sifted names of every worshipped being
for mountains rivers forests were alive
each stone a poem or created thing
separate positive identified
made real by that savage pagan god
who snatched at custody of natural form
bringing new beauty humour or spilt blood
to features of man's ritual concern
so in the eighties we choose modern names
for memorable objects and events
pontificart and popemobile with even
a holycopter for the pope's ascents
humorous to our ears but soon to be
assimilated in the dictionary

29.
after trinity

green hangs for trinity above that chair
where sacristan with patriarchal brow
has left his high-backed seat below the choir
those still-flamed candles hold his memory now
but soon his empty office will be filled
proving that we are all dispensable
the church continuing while under walls
these tragedies intrude and overwhelm
another sunday finds us at this door
stepping across its threshold in new grace
from ritual of bread and wine before
a week's routine slots neatly into place
outside leaf-heavy trees crowding the street
cry green for trinity and paraclete

30.
christening

two seals crack open on our smooth blue phial
then Jordan water trickles into Gwent's
pale daylight while our young protesting child
cries out kicking its robe of falling white
four generations barricade the font
pledged to fulfil promises once made
to guard this glass maintaining a strict bond
between tradition and each given name
bounded by ritual we remember John
who baptised on east river bank all day
waiting to see that bright symbolic dove
of spirit fall out of an empty sky
as holy water dries merging with air
Rhiannon's birds sing at the western door

31.
Peter

Peter free from school leaps to wide beach
drops bursting satchel shoes and anorak
on pebbles out of tide's expected reach
climbs barefoot on one limpet-crusted rock
brass latchkey round his neck proclaims that reign
of flat and sand until late evening call
he hurls stones into sea balanced again
upon his stronghold as burst breakers fall
Peter upon this ancient rock of church
with kingdom's key glistening at his throat
shouts out braving rollers' thunderous lurch
calls to each swiftly passing fishing-boat
three times denying waves that swamp his feet
strong toes grip stone then tide turns in retreat

32.
accident

waiting-room chairs grind upon bare floor
as patients criticise the crawling clock
wheelchairs and stretchers huddle inside door
their blankets folded up in scarlet shock
staggering past a fair-haired youth is led
jeans torn away from leg bleeding and raw
towards one sheeted casualty bed
that dulls his image of electric saw
stark ugliness of torn flesh is displayed
he makes no sound as doctor nurse attend
closing the door then staring and afraid
we are cut off from his appalling wound
left to ourselves we snatch a small reprieve
these injuries are real and we believe

33.
the undefined

stripped and then packaged in my paper robe
I lie prone on this table ringed by eyes
as camera doctor nurse and scanner probe
identity but not my hidden mind
watching these opaque organs which appear
pulsing in monochrome upon lit screen
I see even the detailed spine is there
and am intrigued by my precise machine
normality is hospital's ideal
as proof of health yet the creative act
must be expressed by the unusual
mind that links image word and artefact
inside flat metal plates that slide away
I long to find one poem's clear X-ray

34.
annual fair

red yellow blue these beaded light-bulbs flash
erupting over fairground site at noon
four hundred summers have displayed a brash
festival that transforms our ancient town
again I watch thundering roundabouts
finding emotion overwhelms with pain
as their brief celebration indicates
each pulsing lifespan falters then is gone
this microcosmic world within our world
excites all age-groups with compulsive beat
belts socks and patterned carpet lengths unroll
cascading over baskets at our feet
when morning silence brings us sudden ease
sunlight illuminates unmeasured space

35.
scallop

this brittle scallop washed by tidal flood
contains no remnant of its living being
white fluted layers curve hollow as that void
left by beheaded James when sorrowing
apostles covered up his severed frame
to end those early varied wanderings
now to shell-decorated grottoes come
his modern pilgrims bringing offerings
I find thin skeletons on streaming sand
prise buried fans their smoothness overlaid
raising them dripping in my outspread hand
bone against bone clear radials displayed
while his undrowned and ever-present soul
collects each fragment slowly makes me whole

36.
the gift

in shadowed hours when midnight slips to dawn
sleepless he wanders over Castle hill
expecting nothing to surprise those worn
thoughts that endeavour to wear down his will
thin moon tumbles white above his skull
then in his path a figure formed of light
skims over grass shedding invisible
power that charges him with sudden fright
hallucination dream midsummer glow
cannot explain this vision as it moves
to stare closely under a ragged brow
holding out wounded hands in flowing love
waking painfully on the iron seat
he finds one silver pebble at his feet

37.
cherry-tree garden

flowers then a dove flutter from budded rod
as Joseph takes young Mary for his wife
that secret only she has understood
must overcome his raging disbelief
the new world growing in its holy place
from seed to shoot to slowly opening bloom
forms heavy fruit ripens at quiet pace
so mystery of birth counts out its time
in leafy garden of the cherry-trees
they walk at evening under pleasant shade
'now pick me fruit pull down those cherries please'
but Joseph turns away and leaves the glade
that unborn child commands one rustling tree
'bow down your branches touching Mary's knee'

38.
chapel perilous

the august world crowds out our yellow beach
upon this quest I push my curious way
St. Julian’s chapel perilous is pitched
above grey quaking stones forming the quay
windows are boarded against flooding tide
one candle gleams but organ lid is closed
lettering fades and chalice paten hide
only the cross remains in firm repose
inside closed doors silence begins to soothe
I move towards the altar pause and stare
where that pale knight snatches at linen cloth
then falls to ground as one beam severs air
music rebounds from every rose-red wall
towards his crumpled figure slides the grail

39.
Mary’s house

red leaves fill this grove as autumn creeps
touching the Turkish site of Mary’s house
under old shrines it hid for centuries
until one nun revealed her curious
vision of that deeply layered place
then experts dug in Meryemana bounds
unearthing walls within a sacred glade
expanding history with sudden finds
here was House Beautiful where each new day
she pondered in that upper room called Peace
yet every tree creaking before a gale
reminded her of cross and sacrifice
she died while legend wrapped her gently round
our mother of the world treads holy ground

40.
intercession

intercede for us light under saddle roof
flooding carved figures of long-buried men
intercede for us folded shadow bats
when you awake to circle each bronze bell
intercede for us wafer with raised cross
dissolving on our tongues gently as ashes
out of deep chalice running tilted blood
touches dry lips as slowly the priest passes
gripping high altar rail we take our turn
kneeling between slate floor of lettered stone
and window height to grasp at middle plane
having no wings but fragile hands of bone
filing back to our places in the nave
flesh mind and soaring spirit all believe

41.
for Sybil

her heart fails suddenly as quick impact
of metal against metal blocks the road
home journey incomplete that ritual act
of dying just one second's episode
those layered manuscripts crowning a table
can never be completed by her hand
wide library no longer will be able
to re-live memories of pages signed
such joy in living vanished at a stroke
we send Oxfam donations in despair
but kindled poems remain with careful work
on Newport's poet who would stand and stare
loud laughter lingers round me as I breathe
air of my home-town poorer for her death

42.
loss

where is her bold vitality that burst
into our midst to overflow each crowd
can humour and fierce energy be lost
leaving their body in a sudden flood?
is life-force captured by one newborn child
or merged into green branches' oozing core
why does each movement of an autumn field
ripple with essence of what is no more?
after her funeral coherence fails
so leaving friends I quickly start for home
travelling back through workless towns of Wales
protesting at what cannot be undone
each landmark stabs me with its cruel despair
she only lives in memory and air

43.
climbing in Gwent

at last that summit's brilliant stillness fills
our dazzled senses when we climb its height
lifting our eyes again to Wentwood's hills
hearing one psalm ring out the pilgrim's rite
black ashes of burned bracken stretch away
into flat distance as we stride with gods
upon their plateau passing fallen grey
megaliths in gold-woven lichen shrouds
we rule both fire and air tread covered clay
where probing tongues of green lick cinder death
so resurrection leaps into clear day
and landscape is alive with our quick breath
we stood together on one giant stone
cold ashes blow now I am left alone

44.
harvest festival

we carry ripened produce into church
surround high altar with such brilliant flowers
wide supermarket shelves offered their rich
imported harvest of long labouring hours
so eggs, apples and oranges display
bold curving glory of this contoured earth
while nations of the west greedily pay
for such abundance from exploited wealth
well-fed well-clothed and privileged we kneel
knowing unfairness of our way of ease
with chemicals we have polluted all
these oceans forests and productive fields
forgive then help us all to understand
small harvest needs of every thrust-out hand

45.
walking with angels

archangel Michael paced out Skirrid's ridge
claiming another isolated shrine
for men had raised a chapel near the edge
of that raw fissure slashed to make a sign
on first Good Friday all Gwent's mountains shook
with earthquake tremors through that savage day
but when hewn stones enclosed altar and book
Michael knelt in gold candlelight to pray
curiously we stare where smothered walls
clutch contours underground hide secret acts
of persecuted catholics who crawled
and struggled through september gales to mass
sceptical dare we doubt each past event
walking with angels on blue hills of Gwent?

46.
paradox

one tooth-gap snarls from beeches near the track
as Pembroke's train shakes on its single rail
our ordered cosmos shudders at this lack
of one huge upright touching heaven and hell
Yggdrasill world tree crashed into a field
but gale winds clawing at unsteady root
left me unscathed to travel while they felled
earth's massive form that holds no attribute
of height or grandeur symmetry of leaves
so why does not such violence incite
fierce powers which keep an order in our lives
to rectify their giant oversight?
train carriages command this middle plane
I clutch my luggage dare not look again

47.
autumn sonnet

october of my life is fired with light
that suffering of summer's barrenness
is past and with old energy I fight
through leafy drifts for gold phrases to press
october of my life is sharp with love
piercing our distance with its laser beam
relationships blood-torn when lovers grieve
find retrospect obliterates quick pain
october of my life is blank with sadness
for one lost friend who can no longer find
fresh poems to share while lying on Gwent grass
as I observe new facets of her mind
when equinox fills gales and lashes tide
light love and sadness cluster at my side

48.
Luke’s little summer

heal me as bitter salt washes my wrist
heal me in Luke’s small summer that must fade
heal me as waves slacken each tensioned fist
I tread october beaches at ebb tide
painter and healer moving at my side
you point out marvels in a dogfish skull
green frosted glass with scarlet brick parade
sharp complementaries you take to fill
your palette then one golden citrine stone
trembles beneath my footstep’s detailed print
heal me with colour before winter’s bone
bleaches and creaks so teach me how to paint
these streaming treasures clustered on my shore
preserving texture form and human flaw

49.
All Saints

in concentration camp or lethal rain
our modern saints silently made their stand
starving in dirty cells poisoned with pain
they died for us while nothing new was gained
the world continued on its cruel way
flaunting despair and grim atrocity
yet as each story is revealed today
we glimpse commitment of humanity
one candle flame leaps for each sacrifice
gold pinpricks in thick darkness of our age
we struggle out of present disbelief
leaving deep misery on each smeared page
wax whiteness carries pointed crowns of light
to pierce madness of war's violent night

50.
credo

I believe turning to face the east
where white candles flank one polished cross
that rising sun above creative priest
transforms chalice and white-wafered host
I believe with all these standing friends
who guard emotion under close control
that homage paid when each head gently bends
brings anthem chords to penetrate my soul
I believe while waiting eagle's wings
brace pinions under pages of the word
that truth lingering on as phrasing sings
scatters cadences from an incense cloud
each repetition dazzles with new light
so ancient creed becomes our modern rite

51.
galaxy

this banded galaxy leaps into space
each hazy pinpoint one created world
among the multitudes a unique place
where unimagined properties unfold
and every star shadows another star
as one is part of all and all of one
the whole concept spanning past and future
flaring and dying round its fiery sun
our blind horizon bars us from this sight
on earth’s hurled outpost poems blaze and fade
we catch a visionary glimpse of light
then mind and body build their barricade
so we perform our static sacrament
secure ourselves in this perplexing present

52.
how beautiful

how beautiful on slopes are gripping feet
testing rock surfaces with well-trained skill
seeking that summit where perfection waits
above blue panorama's breathless fall
how beautiful on sand are drifting feet
moving to shifting grains in filling pools
while sea is grinding cliffs to these minute
gold gatherings that stream slowly in ripples
how beautiful on sheets are resting feet
at peace after completion of long toil
entwined or separate each curved instep
arches in glory suddenly immortal
repose perfection transient ritual
elevate spirit over senses' thrill

53.
commandment

do not harm earth or sea or tree until
we have marked every saint upon the brow
do not harm earth inventing ways to kill
and poison land breaking under rough plough
do not harm sea or tree or earth until
we have touched every child upon its mouth
giving it food clean water healing skill
even when ignorance brings fierce rebuff
do not harm tree or earth or sea until
we have filled men and women with new love
helping in age-old struggles as they fail
to make emotions deeply interweave
let every springing thing be glorified
over lost graves of innocents who died

54.
the key

clasping the kingdom’s key I undertake
to gain this city which conceals a town
broad street then lane and yard until I break
long silence of one house standing alone
climbing high stairs I find an open door
enter where a smooth-sheeted bed appears
I long to lie upon its level shore
but touch a resting basket of fresh flowers
who is the flower for annual sacrifice?
what waits below pacing that weedy yard?
where is the newly-sharpened ritual knife
that takes its victim suddenly off-guard?
my head brushes white linen as I pray
for strength to sweep those pagan fears away

55.
incarnation

when wrestling darkness twists us in its grip
hope bursts in the mind so we survive
long advent terror of november sleep
winter imposes on each fragile life
our brain and body struggle through blank hours
preceding dawn then slowly widening light
transforms cool shadows over purple showers
of hangings to a brilliant Christmas white
watching rough wooden crib rock upon straw
excited children lean across this rail
torment of disbelief drops its dead flower
as sun of truth rises dispelling pain
gloom-laden days scatter before that glow
one newborn child dazzles the world we know

56.
Christmas eucharist

the sacramental cycle is complete
advent gives way to word's nativity
easter then whitsun bringing paraclete
hung white and red or green of trinity
families cluster swelling dusted pews
to join in carols' ancient melodies
our glittering priest who welcomed old and new
will celebrate this holy Christmas day
through chantry windows flooding winter light
haloes pale heads of all who file to share
deep crimson blood with body's purest white
raised up and offered to us kneeling here
caught by the brimming cup's compelling power
I gaze into its depths at one gold star